CEC Mini-Library

PERFORMANCE ASSESSMENT

Connecting Performance Assessment to Instruction

Lynn S. Fuchs

Published by
The Council for Exceptional Children

ERIC®

A Product of the
ERIC/OSEP Special Project
The ERIC Clearinghouse on
Disabilities and Gifted Education

Library of Congress Cataloging-in-Publication Data

Fuchs, Lynn,
    Connecting performance assessment to instruction / Lynn S. Fuchs.
    p. cm. — (CEC mini-library performance assessment)
    "A product of the ERIC/OSEP Special Project, the ERIC
Clearinghouse on Disabilities and Gifted Education."
    Includes bibliographical references (p.).
    ISBN 0-86586-248-6
    1. Criterion-referenced tests—Evaluation. 2. Exceptional
children—Rating of. 3. Teaching. I. Council for Exceptional
Children. II. ERIC/OSEP Special Project. III. Title. IV. Series.
LB3060.32.C74F83 1994
371.2'7—dc20   94-17716
                                                                      CIP

ISBN 0-86586-248-6

A product of the ERIC/OSEP Special Project, the ERIC Clearinghouse on Disabilities and Gifted Education

Published in 1994 by The Council for Exceptional Children, 1920 Association Drive, Reston, Virginia 22091-1589

Stock No. P5058

This publication was prepared with funding from the U.S. Department of Education, Office of Special Education Programs, contract no. RR93002005. Contractors undertaking such projects under government sponsorship are encouraged to express freely their judgment in professional and technical matters. Prior to publication the manuscript was submitted for critical review and determination of professional competence. This publication has met such standards. Points of view, however, do not necessarily represent the official view or opinions of either The Council for Exceptional Children or the Department of Education.

Printed in the United States of America

10 9 8 7 6 5 4 3 2

Foreword

CEC's policy on inclusive schools and community settings invites all educators, other professionals, and family members to work together to create early intervention, educational, and vocational programs and experiences that are collegial, inclusive, and responsive to the diversity of children, youth, and young adults. Policymakers at the highest levels of state/provincial and local government, as well as school administration, also must support inclusive principles in the educational reforms they espouse.

One area in which the inclusion of students with disabilities is critical is the development and use of new forms of assessment. This is especially true when assessment becomes a tool by which local school districts, states, and our nation show accountability for the education of students.

As multidimensional instruments that can cross curriculum areas, performance assessments have the potential to be powerful instructional tools as well as tools for accountability. As this new technology is applied in creating new assessment instruments, students with disabilities must be considered during the design of the assessment, administration, scoring, and reporting of results.

CEC is proud to contribute this Mini-Library to the literature on performance assessment, and in so doing to foster the appropiate inclusion of students with disabilities in this emerging technology for instruction and accountability.

Preface

Performance assessment, authentic assessment, portfolio assessment—these are the watchwords of a new movement in educational testing. Its advocates say this movement is taking us beyond the era when the number 2 pencil was seen as an instrument of divine revelation. Its critics say it is just another educational bandwagon carrying a load of untested techniques and unrealistic expectations.

Despite the criticisms and reservations that are sometimes expressed, these new approaches are being implemented in a growing number of large-scale assessment programs at federal, state, and district levels. They are also finding their way into small-scale use at school and classroom levels.

What about students with disabilities? Are the new assessment techniques more valid than conventional assessment techniques for these students? Are the techniques reliable and technically sound? Will they help or hinder the inclusion of students with disabilities in large-scale assessment programs? Can classroom teachers use the techniques to assess student learning and possibly enrich the classroom curriculum?

The following fictional vignettes illustrate some of these issues.

Vignette 1

The State of Yorksylvania developed educational standards and a statewide system of student assessments to monitor progress in achieving the standards. The use of standardized multiple-choice tests was rejected because these tests were thought to trivialize education. It was feared that teachers would "teach down" to the tests rather than "teach up" to the standards. So, committees of teachers, parents, and employers were formed to translate the standards into "authentic" performance assessments. The resulting assessment system was called the Yorksylvania Performance Inventory (YPI).

Once a year, students from every school in the state were administered the YPI, which consisted of several assessments, each of which required up to 3 days to complete. Students worked, sometimes individually and sometimes in small groups, on tests involving complex, high-level tasks that crossed curriculum areas. In one task, students individually did research and answered essay questions interrelating the geography, wildlife, and history of their state. In another task, students worked in groups to design a car powered by fermentation. Schools were provided with practice activities and curriculum guides to encourage the infusion of performance assessment activities into the school curriculum.

The state policy allowed special education students to be included in the YPI, excluded, or provided with special modifications, depending on their individual needs as indicated in their individualized education programs. Initially, most special education teachers supported the YPI because they felt it eliminated some artificial barriers (reading, test-taking skills, etc.) that put their students at a disadvantage on other types of tests. However, there were some questions and issues, such as the following:

- Some of the YPI tasks involved *a lot* of reading, more than was found on previous types of tests.

- Special education teachers sometimes felt pressured to exclude their students from testing in order to increase the school's scores.

- Special education students sometimes experienced extreme frustration in the YPI assessments, many of which bore no resemblance to these students' other schoolwork.

- Some parents of special education students questioned whether the standards were really applicable to their children and whether the YPI was diverting instruction from more relevant and important topics.

Vignette 2

A teacher named Pat had students at a wide range of functioning levels, including a number of mainstreamed students receiving special education services. Pat was always on the lookout for new ideas and approaches. Pat began reading articles and attending conferences on new assessment approaches termed *portfolio assessment, authentic assessment, per-*

formance assessment, and *alternative assessment.* These approaches seemed to make a lot of sense, and Pat decided to try them out. One of the first approaches Pat tried was authentic assessment. Rather than simply testing students on their rote learning of skills and content, Pat began to look for ways to use realistic, complex activities to test whether the students could actually apply what they learned. For example, Pat combined writing, spelling, science, and career skills into an activity in which students wrote letters of application for jobs as physicists, biologists, or chemists. Pat particularly valued activities that engaged students in solving interesting problems. For example, after a unit on optics, Pat assigned students to draw a diagram explaining why mirrors reverse an image from left to right but not from top to bottom. The students grappled with that problem for several days.

Pat liked the holistic scoring procedures developed in these new assessment approaches. Rather than simply marking a response correct or incorrect, Pat scored student work on a number of dimensions (e.g., analysis of the problem, clarity of communication) according to meaningful quality criteria. The development of authentic performance tasks and scoring procedures helped Pat clarify the most important learning outcomes.

Pat also liked the idea of portfolio assessment, in which students could select and collect "best pieces" to demonstrate their learning and achievement during the year. Student self-evaluation became a valued part of this process.

In all, Pat was very pleased with these new assessment approaches and intended to continue using them. Instruction became more activity based and more focused on real-world uses of the material. There were, however, some issues that Pat began to think about:

- Students with deficits in certain academic areas, notably writing, were at a real disadvantage. It was sometimes hard to determine whether an inadequate response resulted from poor writing skills, poor mastery of the content, poor problem-solving skills, lack of creativity, or some combination of these factors. Pat considered allowing some students to tape record their responses, but decided not to. Wasn't writing itself an authentic task required in the real world?

- Pat wasn't sure how to use the information provided by these tests to plan additional instruction, particularly if a student was having difficulty.

- Pat wondered how to tell whether or not an activity was in fact authentic, especially for students whose adult lives would be very different from Pat's own.

In 1992, the Division of Innovation and Development (DID) in the U.S. Department of Education's Office of Special Education Programs and the ERIC/OSEP Special Project of The Council for Exceptional Children formed a Performance Assessment Working Group to discuss issues such as these. The term *performance assessment* was adopted as a general designation for the range of approaches that include performance assessment, authentic assessment, alternative assessment, and portfolio assessment.

Performance assessment was defined has having the following characteristics:

1. *The student is required to create an answer or a product rather than simply fill in a blank, select a correct answer from a list, or decide whether a statement is true or false.*

2. *The tasks are intended to be "authentic."* The conventional approach to test development involves selecting items that represent curricular areas or theoretical constructs, and that have desired technical characteristics (e.g. they correlated with other similar items, they discriminated between groups, etc.). Authentic tasks, on the other hand, are selected because they are "valued in their own right"[1] rather than being "proxies or estimators of actual learning goals."[2]

The Performance Assessment Working Group produced this series of four Mini-Library books on various topics related to performance assessment and students with disabilities. In *National and State Perspectives on Performance Assessment and Students with Disabilities,* Martha Thurlow discusses trends in the use of performance assessment in large-scale testing programs. In *Performance Assessment and Students with Disabilities: Usage in Outcomes-Based Accountability Systems,* Margaret McLaughlin and Sandra Hopfengardner Warren describe the experi-

---

[1] R. L. Linn, E. L. Baker, & S. B. Dunbar. (1991). Complex, performance-based assessment: Expectations and validation criteria. *Educational Researcher, 20*(8), 15–21.
[2] M. W. Kirst. (1991). Interview on assessment issues with Lorrie Shepard. *Educational Researcher, 20*(2), 21–23, 27.

ences of state and local school districts in implementing performance assessment. In *Creating Meaningful Performance Assessments: Fundamental Concepts*, Stephen Elliott discusses some of the key technical issues involved in the use of performance assessment. And, in *Connecting Performance Assessment to Instruction*, Lynn Fuchs discusses the classroom use of performance assessment by teachers.

Martha J. Coutinho
University of Central Florida

David B. Malouf
U.S. Office of Special Education Programs

August, 1994

Members of the Performance Assessment Work Group

Joan Baron, Performance Assessment Collaborative for Education, Harvard University

Joyce Choate, Council for Exceptional Diagnostic Services, Northeast Louisiana University

Lorraine Costella, Frederick County, Maryland, Public Schools

Martha Coutinho, Division of Innovation and Development, U.S. Office of Special Education Programs

Stephen Elliott, University of Wisconsin-Madison

Lynn Fuchs, Vanderbilt University

John Haigh, Maryland State Department of Education

Larry Irvin, University of Oregon

Robert Linn, Center for Research on Evaluation, Standards, and Student Testing

Lynn Malarz, Association for Supervision and Curriculum Development

David Malouf, Division of Innovation and Development, U.S. Office of Special Education Programs

Margaret McLaughlin, Center for Policy Options in Special Education, University of Maryland

Trina Osher, National Association of State Directors of Special Education

James Poteet, Council for Educational Diagnostic Services, Ball State University

Clay Starlin, Western Regional Resource Center, University of Oregon

Martha Thurlow, National Center on Educational Outcomes for Students with Disabilities, University of Minnesota

Sandra Hopfengardner Warren, Center for Policy Options in Special Education, University of Maryland

Note. Members' affiliations may have changed since the work group was formed.

About the Author

Well-known among the special education research community for her work in curriculum-based measurement (CBM), **Lynn S. Fuchs** believes that her interest in CBM led naturally to her desire to explore the instructional possibilities of performance-based assessment. "CBM meets many of the criteria that educators are looking for in new technologies of assessment. I am interested in how teachers can best use assessment information and the forms in which it can be obtained and presented to them to allow them to use it to maximum advantage. It will be exciting to see what new assessment and instructional technologies emerge from current trends in education."

Dr. Fuchs's work with children who have special needs began when she was an undergraduate at Johns Hopkins University. She served as a tutor for children who were incarcerated, many of whom had significant learning problems. As a result of this experience, she became interested in education in general, especially for children from low-income, underprivileged backgrounds. As undergraduates, she and her husband, Doug, began a Saturday school for neighborhood children. The school was quite popular and grew into a summer program in Baltimore.

She attended the University of Pennsylvania to prepare for her certification in elementary education and then taught first grade. She later obtained her special education certification in Minneapolis and taught students with mild learning problems. As she taught, she attended the University of Minnesota and participated in some of the studies conducted by its Institute for Research in Learning Disabilities. After serving as a resource teacher in the Minneapolis Public Schools for 5 years, she completed her Ph.D. at the University of Minnesota and devoted her career to research.

Teachers' use of assessment systems has been Dr. Fuchs's continuing research interest. Over the years, her projects have focused on teachers' planning and adapting instruction for classes of diverse students, peer-mediated instruction, and ways of helping children interact with each other in constructive ways. Her work has evolved to take its current focus: merging CBM and peer-mediated instruction to help teachers organize their classes to accommodate diverse students. Through this work, she is creating a vehicle by which classrooms can be reorganized to allow assessments to be of greater usefulness to teachers.

Dr. Fuchs is currently Professor in the Department of Special Education and Co-Director of the Institute on Education and Learning in the Kentucky Center for Research on Human Development at the Peabody College of Vanderbilt University. Her work has been published extensively.

Contents

1. Introduction

A major goal of the current education reform movement is to enhance teacher instruction and student performance on tasks that reflect the requirements of the real world. This emphasis on authentic performance translates into a need for students to demonstrate problem solving, comprehension, writing, critical thinking, and metacognitive skills. To (a) concretize the problematic emphasis of the past on basic, factual content and (b) conceptualize the idealistic visions for the future on authentic performances, many leaders of the reform movement have fixed their attention on testing and assessment.

The key features of traditional commercial achievement tests make them easy targets for criticism (see, for example, Archbald & Newmann, 1988; Linn, 1991; Shepard, 1989; Wiggins, 1989). The testing domains are limited largely to basic and factual information; the assessment formats stress individual achievement, whereas modern workplaces often demand cooperation; the test items do not require students to synthesize knowledge across domains; and the tests rely almost exclusively on multiple-choice response formats.

Despite these valid criticisms, most measurement experts agree that scores based on traditional commercial achievement tests correlate highly with important criterion measures. For example, research indicates that multiple-choice tests can predict performance on essay tests as well as or better than other essay tests and that multiple-choice tests are better predictors of grades than are essay tests (see Linn, 1991). Given this strong predictive validity of traditional commercial achievement tests, why the continued calls for assessment reform?

The answer may be found in a relatively recent phenomenon, high stakes testing, whereby scores are used to formulate judgments about the quality of schools and districts, the effectiveness of individual teachers, and in some cases the allocation of educational funds or personnel. When the consequences of traditional commercial achievement testing are serious, the content of tests begins to influence what teachers teach and what students learn. That is, the content of the commercial achievement tests begins to *direct* instruction. When teachers, in preparing their students to perform well on end-of-year tests, tailor the curriculum to emphasize basic, factual information, stress individual achievement over cooperation, deemphasize synthesis of knowledge across disciplines, and rely heavily on multiple-choice response formats, educational quality suffers.

But what about the role of teacher-made tests that assess students' mastery of the classroom's curriculum? Unfortunately, analyses of teacher-constructed tests (e.g., Fleming & Chambers, 1983; Stiggins, Griswald, & Green, 1988) indicate that most questions require simple recall of factual information rather than synthesis, comparison, or analysis. It is unclear whether this factual content reflects the desire to mimic and teach to commercial achievement tests or teachers are driven by the same motivation as commercial test developers for efficiency in scoring and test interpretation. In either case, however, the result is that many students have relatively few opportunities in school to practice, master, and demonstrate the kinds of complex thinking required in the real world.

Consequently, a major impetus for the performance assessment movement has been the need to reconnect large-scale and classroom-based assessment to learning so that assessment affects learning positively. This book explores how a synergy between assessment and instruction can be forged to enhance student outcomes, especially for students with disabilities.

Chapter 2 defines and discusses assessment that enhances instruction and provides an overview of important criteria for judging the utility of this type of assessment. Chapter 3 describes previous efforts within special education to link assessment and instruction to improve teacher planning and decision making. The strengths and limitations of these methods are discussed.

Chapter 4 introduces performance assessment as a newer alternative for strengthening the connection between assessment and instruction. A case study illustrates a teacher's use of performance assessment during instructional decision making. Finally, Chapter 5 discusses how performance assessment addresses the criteria for ensuring a tight connection between assessment and instruction. Key areas requiring additional development and research are noted.

A major impetus for the performance assessment movement has been the need to reconnect large-scale and classroom-based assessment to learning so that assessment affects learning positively.

---

2. Instructionally Linked Assessment

Definition and Purposes

For this book, Nitko's definition of testing as "any systematic procedure for observing and classifying students' performance for the purpose of obtaining instructionally relevant information" (1989, p. 447) has been adopted. The discussion here is restricted to teachers' use of "internal tests," which are used to make day-to-day instructional decisions. The use of "external tests," which are created, imposed, and controlled by agencies outside a teacher's school, is discussed in other books in this series on performance assessment (see McLaughlin & Warren, *Performance Assessment and Students with Disabilities: Usage in Outcomes-Based Accountability Systems*, and Thurlow, *National and State Perspectives on Performance Assessment and Students with Disabilities*).

With ongoing evaluative feedback, teachers can improve their responsiveness to students and increase the effectiveness of their instruction.

At least four benefits can be realized from integrating instructional decision making with assessment. Student motivation for and involvement in learning may increase through enhanced feedback. Teachers may be better informed of both the learning progress and the difficulties of their students. The effectiveness of instruction may be evaluated accurately. Finally, with ongoing evaluative feedback, teachers may improve their responsiveness to individual students and increase the effectiveness of their instruction.

Three types of decisions are important points of focus for instructionally oriented assessment: instructional placement decisions, formative evaluation decisions, and diagnostic decisions. Instructional placement decisions determine the point within an instructional sequence where a student should begin in order to avoid unnecessary repetition of material the student already knows or frustrating exposure to material beyond the student's grasp.

With formative evaluation, a teacher uses ongoing assessment to monitor a student's learning while an instructional program is under way. From the learner's perspective, formative evaluation provides ongoing feedback, so the student can become purposeful and goal oriented in learning. For the teacher, it provides information for determining how quickly progress is being made, judging whether or not the instructional program is effective, and deciding when a change in the instructional program is necessary to promote better learning.

Diagnostic assessment typically occurs after formative evaluation has indicated inadequate student learning. Diagnostic decisions determine which specific difficulties account for a student's inadequate progress so that the teacher can remediate the learning problem and design more effective instructional plans. The form and focus of diagnostic assessment vary with conceptual orientation. Diagnostic methods vary widely (see Nitko, 1989). For example, approaches based on *trait profile differences* define deficits as low standings relative to other children on broad learning outcomes. Approaches based on *prerequisite knowledge and skills deficits* identify the skills or knowledge a student has failed to acquire within a learning hierarchy. Approaches based on *erroneous behavior identification* seek to determine the types of incorrect responses that are interfering with efficient learning. *Knowledge structure* approaches define deficits as incorrect cognitive strategies or conceptual organizations.

Criteria and Principles

In considering assessments that inform instructional decisions, the following criteria and principles apply (see Table 1). The assessments should:

1. *Measure important learning outcomes.* Assessment methods must be aligned with important learning outcomes. *Important* means that students perform competently inside or outside of classrooms on novel tasks that require them to combine subskills into integrated performances.

2. *Address three assessment purposes.* Desirable assessment techniques produce information that can satisfy more than one of the three decision-making functions (i.e., instructional placement, formative evaluation, and diagnosis of learning problems). Assessment methods that can address multiple functions allow teachers to operate more efficiently and effectively.

3. *Provide clear descriptions of student performance that can be linked to instructional actions.* Assessments should yield rich and highly detailed analyses of student performance that connect clearly and immediately to specific instructional decisions. Some analyses of student performance are more functional than others for making instructional decisions. For example, an analysis that categorizes reading errors in terms of omissions, substitutions, and additions can be difficult to translate into a productive teaching technique. By contrast, an analysis that organizes reading errors in terms of phonetic categories (e.g., student produces short vowel sound in consonant-vowel-consonant-e words) relates well to an instructional strategy (e.g., use mnemonics to teach the student the related phonics rule).

4. *Be compatible with a variety of instructional models.* One assessment method should permit a teacher to use and evaluate different instructional approaches. An assessment framework should not dictate one type of instructional program or limit a teacher's options for experimenting with varying methods.

5. *Be feasible.* Classroom-based assessment methods must be easily administered, scored, and interpreted by teachers. In addition, the instructional decisions made on the basis of the assessment must be manageable in everyday classroom life.

6. *Communicate the goals of learning to teachers and students.* Instructionally relevant assessment should serve as a vehicle for communicating what is important to learn. After reviewing the content, process, and format of the assessment instruments they will use over the course of the year, teachers should be able to plan their instruction to improve student scores on the assessments. If the assessments reflect the desired learning outcomes and are broad enough to tap generalized learning, then it should be beneficial to plan instruction to enhance students' performance on assessments. In addition, as students become familiar with the structure of their assessments and the criteria by which their performance will be judged, the goals of the instructional program should become clear and their understanding of where to focus their effort should increase.

Assessment methods incorporated into an instructional process must contribute to the student's motivation for learning. Well-designed assessment methods may increase students' interest in learning, orient them to establish personal learning goals and seek help to achieve those goals, enhance the relevancy of the instructional content to the students' own concerns, and increase their satisfaction with school. Prior research (Dornbusch & Scott, 1975; Natriello & Dornbusch, 1984) suggests that assessment can stimulate student effort when students perceive a close connection between assessments and future success or social approval, when they experience a relationship between their effort and improvement on the assessments over time, and when they believe the assessments are fair.

7. *Generate accurate, meaningful information.* Instructionally focused assessment methods should produce accurate, meaningful information that is sensitive to student improvement. Elliott's book in this series (*Creating Meaningful Performance Assessments: Fundamental Concepts*) addresses related points. Suffice it to say here that the need to produce information that meets established technical standards often is overlooked when assessment information is collected for the purpose of informing instructional decisions (Tindal et al., 1985). Sound instructional decisions cannot be formulated on the basis of idiosyncratic, erroneous information.

TABLE 1
Criteria and Principles Applied to Well-Established Assessment Traditions in Special Education

	Assessment Tradition		
Criterion/Principle	Behavioral Assessment	Mastery Learning	Curriculum-Based Measurement
Measures important outcomes			X
Satisfies three purposes	X	X	X
Provides clear descriptions linked to instructional actions	X		
Is compatible with many instructional models			X
Is feasible	X		X
Communicates learning goals to teachers and students	X	X	X
Generates accurate, meaningful information	X		X

X indicates that the method satisfies the criterion or principle.

3. Previous Efforts to Link Assessment to Instruction

Due to the serious learning problems of students with disabilities, the field of special education has a longstanding history of developing innovative methods to link student performance information to instructional planning. At least three assessment methods used within special education attempt to link assessment to instruction in constructive ways: behavioral assessment, mastery learning, and curriculum-based measurement. This chapter summarizes the key features of each method, briefly illustrates its use, and discusses the extent to which the method satisfies the criteria by which alternative assessment methods are judged.

Behavioral Assessment

Key Features

Defined as "the direct observation and recording of a subject's target behaviors by an observer under the stimulus control of a written behavior code" (Baer, Wolf, & Risley, 1987, p. 316), behavioral assessment has four fundamental characteristics. First, it relies on direct measurement; that is, the assessment focuses on the problem behavior in the setting in which the behavior occurs. Second, it incorporates repeated measurement. Data from repeated measurements are analyzed over time, in terms of level, slope, variability, step changes, and percentage of nonoverlap, to yield information about the student's learning. Third, behavioral assessment and the principles of the experimental analysis of behavior are connected intimately. "Baseline logic" is used to judge the merit of an intervention strategy by comparing an individual's performance under varying, controlled conditions (Tawney & Gast, 1984). Fourth, various environmental factors are examined for their effect on behavior. These situational variables are believed to influence behavior during the assessment process, and their analysis and manipulation are linked to the development of intervention programs (Kratochwill & Shapiro, 1988).

Illustration

To illustrate how behavioral assessment is implemented in special education programs, let us consider Fred, a hypothetical adolescent with severe cognitive impairments who is having difficulty shopping in the supermarket. His teacher, Mr. Craft, accompanies Fred to the supermarket to observe him shopping. As he observes Fred informally, Mr. Craft conducts a task analysis to determine 12 component skills that comprise supermarket shopping and orders these skills from first to last in a sequence required for successful completion of the task. Then, for each skill, Mr. Craft creates an operational definition and designs a strategy for measuring Fred's mastery.

Mr. Craft identifies the first three skills in this hierarchy as (1) creating a complete list of items to be purchased, (2) identifying where in the supermarket these items can be found, and (3) identifying the lowest price for each item. To measure performance on these skills, Mr. Craft frames the following behavioral objectives, which define the assessment strategies:

1. When told a story involving 10 items to be purchased at the supermarket, Fred will create a list of words or icons correctly representing the 10 items.

2. For each of 10 items on a list, Fred will go to the correct aisle, within 3 feet of the item.

3. Given a list of 10 items, Fred will write the lowest price next to each item.

Before beginning instruction, Mr. Craft takes baseline data on each skill on 5 consecutive days. He enlists the assistance of the instructional aide to take data simultaneously so that he will have an estimate of the reliability or accuracy of these assessments. These baseline scores for each of the three skills are graphed in Figure 1.

Fred's performance is relatively consistent, or stable, on each skill, so Mr. Craft begins instruction on the first skill. He teaches Fred icons and words to represent 50 common supermarket items. He works with Fred to sift through shopping narratives to identify which products need to be purchased and to transfer a symbol for each item to a list as it is identified. Hence, the instruction is linked closely to the measurement strategy. Following each day's lesson, Mr. Craft measures Fred's performance on each of the three skills and scores and graphs Fred's

FIGURE 1
Fred's Shopping Behaviors Over Time
(Number correct on number of items on shopping list, number of
items correctly found, and number of items correctly priced)

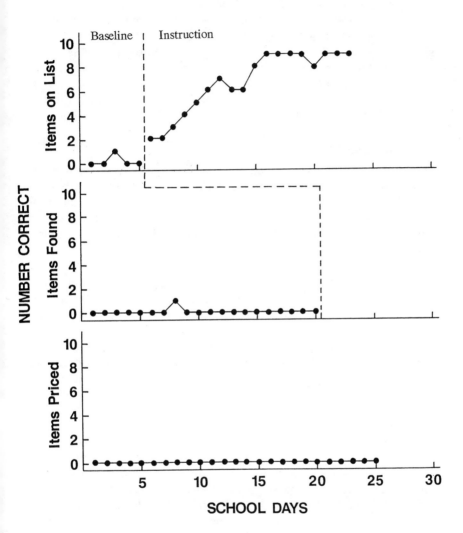

performances. He compares Fred's baseline data on the first skill (i.e., the first 5 points on the top panel) to the intervention data (i.e., the next 14 points on the top panel) and concludes that Fred has mastered the skill of making a shopping list. Mr. Craft also compares Fred's improvement on the two remaining skills and determines that Fred has not mastered the untaught material. Because Fred has shown improvement on the taught skill and has not demonstrated change on the untaught skills, Mr. Craft concludes that Fred's growth on the taught skill is a *function* of the instruction provided. After Fred's demonstration of mastery on the first skill, Mr. Craft refocuses instruction on the second skill in the sequence. He proceeds to measure and teach each skill in the sequence until all 12 skills are mastered.

Strengths and Limitations

Over the years, special educators have relied heavily on behavioral assessment to plan, monitor, and improve programs for students with disabilities. Behavioral assessment has enjoyed a strong record as a tool for improving the connection between assessment and instruction in constructive ways that enhance instructional decisions and student achievement.

Behavioral assessment satisfies five criteria for assessment. As an early forerunner of assessment methods in which a tight connection exists between assessment and instruction, behavioral assessment satisfies some of the key criteria for instructionally relevant assessment listed in Chapter 2. For example, behavioral assessment can simultaneously inform placement, formative evaluation, and diagnostic decisions. Its use of task analysis facilitates placement decisions by identifying where in the sequence a student can profit most from instruction; its reliance on repeated measurement of an individual's behavior and on baseline logic to judge the effects of treatment makes it well suited for formative evaluation; and its close analysis of the environment within which behavior is demonstrated can yield fruitful diagnostic decisions to enhance performance. In addition, behavioral assessment communicates clearly to teachers and students what the essential learning content is; it has established high standards for the reliability of the measurement; and it is relatively feasible for teachers to implement in the special settings within which it is typically employed.

Behavioral assessment tends to focus on discrete tasks that do not necessarily sum to important outcomes. As discussed by Baer and colleagues (1987), within behavioral assessment, "Valid measurement is measurement of . . . [the] behavior that has caused the problem-presenter to present it"

(p. 316). Thus, a key criterion for judging the integrity of an assessment is its accurate representation of the presenting problem or the outcome desired for the individual. Consequently, behavioral assessments are designed to match instructional goals, and the validity of those assessments is judged by their representation of desired outcomes. In this way, behavioral assessment strives to target important outcomes.

The theoretical underpinnings of behavioral assessment, however, limit its focus to observable behaviors. Although this focus contributes to behavioral assessment's strong measurement precision, it sometimes can also result in practitioners' separating complicated behaviors into their component parts and then measuring (and teaching to) relatively small instructional chunks. These small units, observed and measured in isolation, can be difficult for students to piece together and apply to real-world contexts.

For example, when a student exhibits difficulties, a behaviorally oriented framework frequently leads to a task-analytic approach. As shown in the case just described, Mr. Craft relied on task analysis to determine that shopping in the supermarket comprised 12 component skills. He ordered these skills and assessed Fred's performance on each one. He then determined that the first skill Fred failed to perform proficiently was creating a shopping list. He began instruction on this subskill and measured Fred's proficiency on this and two additional, closely sequenced skills each day. When Fred mastered the instructional target, Mr. Craft shifted instruction to the next component skill and so on until Fred had mastered each one.

Although this approach appears logical in its attempt to separate a complicated, multidimensional performance into its subparts and teach those more manageable parts one at a time, research suggests that students, especially those with learning problems, often fail to integrate subparts into authentic performances and to transfer their learning to other settings (Anderson-Inman, Walker, & Purcell, 1984; White, 1984). Therefore, to extend this example, although Fred might master all 12 component skills, he also might fail to put these 12 behaviors together in an integrated way. That is, Fred might still be unable to shop in the supermarket, and the assessment would not reveal his more molar difficulty.

This limitation of behavioral assessment has been recognized by its adherents (e.g., Baer et al., 1987), and efforts have been made to develop methods that facilitate integration of subparts and enhance generalization. Nevertheless, this limitation remains a serious problem, and disagreement persists about the extent to which behavioral assessment meets the criterion of measuring important outcomes that reflect performances inside and outside of classrooms—especially on novel tasks that require integrated performances across subskills.

Behavioral assessment limits the teacher's choice of instructional approaches. This focus on discrete behaviors and the resulting close connection between the assessment system and the model of instruction limit the range of instructional decisions that a teacher can make. A behavioral assessment framework dictates a behaviorally oriented instructional program that is directed at discrete behaviors and incorporates an applied behavior-analytic framework. Consequently, the measurement limits the range of instructional treatments that may be considered.

A behavioral assessment framework dictates an . . . instructional program that is oriented toward discrete behaviors.

Mastery Learning

Features

In *A Model of School Learning,* Carroll (1963) proposed that the amount a student learns in school is a function of time spent and time needed to learn. That is, given sufficient opportunity to learn (or allocated quality instructional time) and time actually spent learning (i.e., engaged time), the majority of children should achieve some specified criterion level of performance. Bloom (1976) operationalized this conceptual model into a unified assessment and instructional system known as *mastery learning.*

With mastery learning, a global curriculum is broken down into a set of subskills, which then are ordered into a hierarchy of instructional objectives. For each step in the instructional hierarchy, a criterion-referenced test is designed and a performance criterion is specified for inferring mastery of the subskill. The teacher moves to the lowest step in the hierarchy, pretests students on that skill, teaches the objective, and posttests students on the material. If a student does not demonstrate mastery, the teacher applies corrective strategies until the student achieves mastery of the learning unit. When mastery is demonstrated, the teacher advances the student to the next, more difficult step in the hierarchy.

Through this process of periodic assessment combined with systematic correction of individual learning difficulties, each student should receive appropriate amounts of allocated quality instructional time and engaged learning time. Bloom (1976) reasoned that, under

---

these conditions, virtually all students could achieve mastery of school curricula.

Illustration

Ms. Fox, a first-grade teacher, specifies a learning hierarchy that begins with grapheme–phoneme associations, continues with consonant–vowel–consonant phonetically patterned words, proceeds to final-e patterned words, and so on. For each step in the hierarchy, Ms. Fox designs a criterion-referenced assessment (e.g., for grapheme–phoneme associations, presenting the child with randomly ordered flashcards containing graphemes and requiring the child to say the corresponding phonemes). At the beginning of the school year, Ms. Fox pretests her students on the first skill in the hierarchy using this measurement strategy. For students who demonstrate mastery (26 of 26 phonemes correct), Ms. Fox assesses performance of the next, more difficult skill. For students who do not show mastery, she delivers her instructional unit on grapheme–phoneme associations. After delivering this unit, she reassesses the students. For children who continue to have difficulty, Ms. Fox implements a corrective strategy. For those who demonstrate mastery, instruction and assessment simultaneously shift to the next skill in the hierarchy. For each step in the hierarchy, therefore, the teacher pretests the students, implements an instructional unit, and then posttests the students. Depending on the posttest performance, the teacher either moves to the next skill in the hierarchy or cycles through an instructional unit before testing again.

Strengths and Limitations

Research has documented that mastery learning can be incorporated into all levels of schooling, from preschool curricula to college courses, with positive effects (Bloom, 1976). In terms of the criteria presented in Chapter 2 for judging the acceptability and utility of an assessment approach for instructional planning, mastery learning satisfies two key principles. First, like behavioral assessment, mastery learning addresses the three purposes of assessment: (1) Its reliance on task analysis creates a structure for identifying profitable instructional placements for students; (2) its episodic schedule for reassessment provides a framework for formative evaluation; and (3) its careful observations of students during assessments facilitate the development of diagnostic plans for addressing specific student difficulties. In addition, mastery learning communicates simply and directly to both teachers and students about what is important to teach and learn.

Mastery learning can lead to mastery of isolated skills without achievement of the more important outcomes. Mastery learning suffers from the same limitation as behavioral assessment. That is, it focuses on discrete behaviors in both assessment and instruction. Unfortunately, although mastery learning assumes that students will combine these behaviors into integrated performances, students—especially those with disabilities— often fail to integrate the parts and generalize to more natural contexts (Anderson-Inman et al., 1984; White, 1984).

Extending the earlier example, although a student with learning problems may demonstrate the capacity to read separate lists of words, each of which contains one type of phonetic pattern, he or she may fail to read more natural text that mixes words with different phonetic patterns. Consequently, a measurement focus on discrete steps in a learning hierarchy can cause the teacher to overestimate the student's real learning. It also can limit instructional domains to unnatural, decontextualized tasks, thereby orienting the assessment to less important outcomes.

Mastery learning limits the teacher's instructional options. Like behavioral assessment, the mastery learning approach to assessment dictates a particular instructional method; that is, it requires mastery of a particular behavior before teachers can expose students to subsequent skills. This approach can restrict a teacher's instructional options, limiting the kinds of analyses of student performance and the range of instructional decisions the teacher can use.

Mastery learning does not meet established technical assessment standards. The other limitations of mastery learning stand in stark contrast to the important strengths of behavioral assessment: Mastery learning fails to incorporate behavioral assessment's emphasis on reliable, repeated measurement, clear rules of evidence, and a thorough analysis of the environment to design effective interventions.

Specifically, within mastery learning, relatively little emphasis has been placed on the reliability or validity of assessment methods. Teachers typically design their own criterion-referenced tests without concern for the accuracy, precision, or meaningfulness of the resulting database. Even commercial criterion-referenced tests fail to meet accepted standards for reliability and validity (Tindal et al., 1985). Consequently, users do not know what exactly is being assessed, how to interpret the resulting information, and how to use the measures effectively.

In addition, the frequency with which students are assessed is unclear. Typically, the teacher administers a pretest prior to an instructional unit and reassesses students only after instructional units are completed. Students cannot advance to more difficult steps in the hierarchy when they actually achieve mastery; they must wait until the teacher provides the opportunity for demonstrating mastery during reassessment. Thus, the "repeated" nature of mastery learning is relatively infrequent, it affords few opportunities for advancement by the student or corrective action by the teacher.

Mastery learning does not clearly connect assessment results with instructional actions. At least as it is actually practiced by teachers, mastery learning's rules for dealing with student failure are loose. It is not uncommon for teachers to require students who demonstrate mastery at pretest to complete instructional units or to advance students to more difficult instructional steps despite their failure to show mastery during posttesting (Fuchs, Tindal, & Fuchs, 1986).

Mastery learning cannot summarize student learning efficiently and can be infeasible for practitioners. Because the focus of measurement changes each time a student achieves mastery of a step in the curriculum, and because steps in the curriculum are of unequal difficulty, progress cannot be judged or described over extended periods of time. Moreover, because different students need to be measured simultaneously on different steps of the curriculum, mastery learning systems can become unmanageable for teachers under routine classroom conditions.

Curriculum-Based Measurement

Features

Developed over the past decade under the leadership of Stanley L. Deno at the University of Minnesota, curriculum-based measurement is an example of a broader class of assessment known as *general outcome measurement.* The purpose of general outcome measurement is to provide teachers with reliable, valid, and efficient procedures for obtaining student performance data to evaluate their instructional programs and to answer broad questions such as "How effective is my instructional program in producing growth over time and in comparison to other instructional strategies I might use with this child?"

In developing a general outcome measurement system, Deno and his colleagues incorporated two key assessment features (see Fuchs & Deno, 1991 for discussion). First, the measurement methods are standardized; that is, both the critical behaviors to be measured and the procedures for measuring those behaviors are prescribed. Second, the focus of the measurement is long term: The testing methods and content remain constant across relatively long time periods, such as 1 year.

Prescriptive procedures and long-range consistency, therefore, are the distinctive features of curriculum-based measurement.

In using curriculum-based measurement, for example, a teacher establishes a broad long-term outcome for the student such as performing mathematics at the third-grade level competently. Then, instead of specifying a hierarchy of subskills that comprise the third-grade mathematics curriculum and measuring student performance one skill at a time, as might be done within a behavioral assessment or mastery learning framework, the teacher relies on well-established curriculum-based measurement methods for measuring student proficiency in mathematics on the entire third-grade curriculum.

Specifically, the teacher creates a pool of equivalent assessments, each of which samples the key problem types from the third-grade curriculum in the same proportion. Each week, the teacher has the student complete one or two assessments. At the beginning of the year, the student completes few problems correctly. As the year progresses and the curriculum is taught, however, the student's performance should gradually improve.

Because each assessment is of equal difficulty and incorporates all the important types of problems to be learned over the course of the year, the curriculum-based measurement database produces two types of information. First, a total score on the assessment is graphed over time to indicate overall progress. The purpose of the graphed presentation of total scores is to allow teachers and students to evaluate overall growth formatively. Second, an analysis of the student's performance on the subskills embedded in the curriculum can be conducted to allow the teacher and student to engage in diagnostic problem solving—that is, to determine how to improve the instructional program. In essence, curriculum-based measurement combines traditional methods of test construction, validation, interpretation, and use with more specific, defined, and instructionally useful concepts and techniques associated with alternative assessment methods.

Illustration

Mrs. Sail, a special education resource teacher, is working with a sixth-grade boy, George, who has an identified learning disability in mathematics. Mrs. Sail, who has adopted a curriculum-based measurement orientation, has determined that an appropriate goal for George is that he master the fourth-grade mathematics curriculum this year. With this goal in mind, Mrs. Sail relies on standardized curriculum-based measurement methods to sample her school's fourth-grade mathematics curriculum. This provides her with 30 alternate test forms, each of which samples the same types of problems in the same proportion.

Mrs. Sail begins by estimating George's current performance level on this material: She uses standard methods to administer three assessments on three different days. Figure 2 is a graph showing George's total scores on these assessments over time. His initial assessments indicate that he scores approximately 10 points correct on the fourth-grade curriculum. Based on norm-referenced criteria, Mrs. Sail sets an ambitious goal of 1 point per week. Because 30 weeks remain in the school year, Mrs. Sail establishes an end-of-year goal of 40 points correct (an initial score of 10 plus 30). On Figure 2, the vertical broken line indicates when the goal was set; the G (signifying the goal) is placed at the intersection of May 15 and 40 points; and a dotted diagonal line represents the approximate rate of improvement George must demonstrate in order to achieve the goal.

After estimating the initial performance level and setting the end-of-year goal, Mrs. Sail begins to implement her instructional program. Twice weekly, she administers a curriculum-based measurement using standard methods for administration and scoring. The fourth through twelfth points on Figure 2 show the scores George earns while Mrs. Sail is implementing this program (see middle portion of the graph). The actual rate of progress (i.e., the solid line through these points) is flatter than the desired rate of progress. Through this formative evaluation, Mrs. Sail determines that her instructional program is not producing the desired effects and that she needs to adjust that program.

To diagnose profitable strategies to adjusting the program, Mrs. Sail inspects George's skills profile (see bottom portion of Figure 2). Based on this skills analysis, she decides to modify her instructional program in the following ways. George has improved his performance on the measurement portions of the curriculum. As indicated by the striped boxes becoming checkered boxes, his accuracy has increased over time—although his fluency is still too low to warrant mastery (see *Me*, which stands for Measurement, on the third row of the skills analysis). Consequently, Mrs. Sail decides to provide drill and practice on this material to increase George's fluency. In addition, because George has achieved mastery on applied computation (AP), she decides to vary the drill and practice activities so that each exercise includes both measurement and applied computation problems. Finally, given George's continued low accuracy on charts and graphs (see fourth row, CG), she decides to provide initial instructional activities on this material.

The solid vertical line in Figure 2 indicates that the instructional program is modified at the end of October. As shown in the next eight points, George's performance improves with the institution of this adjustment. The actual rate of progress is steeper than the desired rate of improvement; thus, Mrs. Sail decides to raise her goal.

FIGURE 2
Curriculum-Based Measurement Graph (top) and Skills Profile (bottom), Showing George's Progress Over Time on the Fourth-Grade Curriculum

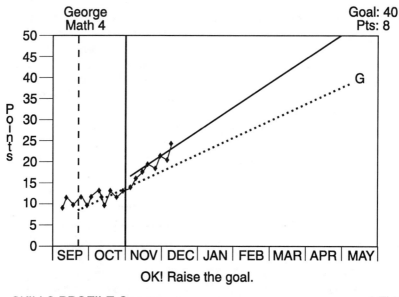

OK! Raise the goal.

Note: The skills profile corresponds to the end of October, when George's progress was less than satisfactory, not early December, when George's progress has improved. The rows represent the different skills embedded in the fourth-grade curriculum; the columns represent half-month intervals of the school year. Boxes are coded as follows: Black boxes indicate mastery; black boxes with a dot, probable mastery; gridded boxes, partial mastery; striped boxes, nonmastery; empty boxes, nonattempted.

Strengths and Limitations

Curriculum-based measurement satisfies six criteria for assessments. Because curriculum-based measurement incorporates standard measurement techniques based on reliability and validity research, it provides an accurate and meaningful database. In addition, its regular schedule for assessment and its focus on the year-long curriculum allow curriculum-based measurement to address the three purposes of assessment. For example, in identifying the year-end goal, the teacher can simultaneously formulate an instructional placement decision. The graphed information also summarizes an individual's overall progress on the year's curriculum and therefore can be used to evaluate progress formatively and determine when a change in the instructional program is warranted. Additionally, curriculum-based measurement's skills analysis offers rich and detailed information about a student's performance on specific skills and can be used diagnostically to determine how to improve the instructional program.

Moreover, expert system computer programs have been developed (e.g., Fuchs, Fuchs, Hamlett, & Ferguson, 1992; Fuchs, Fuchs, Hamlett, & Stecker, 1991) to link the diagnostic information to specific instructional recommendations, enhancing teachers' capacity to benefit from the assessment profiles. Another feature of curriculum-based measurement that enhances its benefits for teachers is that, unlike behavioral assessment and mastery learning, the measurement framework is not tied to any particular model of instruction. Therefore, there is a broad range of instructional options associated with this assessment method. The teachers are not tied to any particular sequence with which to introduce skills, and they are not committed to mastery of any individual skills before moving to different instructional material. A teacher can use widely varying methods with the same child to determine which method is most beneficial.

The scoring criteria are open and clear, so that students know how they are evaluated and can set personal learning goals, and the structure of the assessment can help teachers identify teaching content. In addition, the assessment demands are relatively manageable for teachers in ordinary classroom settings because of three factors. First, curriculum-based measurement was developed with a deliberate focus on efficiency, so that the assessments are brief. Second, the focus of the assessment remains consistent across relatively long time periods, so that teachers do not have to shift assessments for different students at different times. Finally, because well-developed computer programs automatically administer assessments and manage and analyze the assessment database, teachers can be freed from virtually all of the mechanical tasks associated with the administration, scoring, and management of assessments.

Curriculum-based measurement's broad focus on integrated performances may limit its connections to instructional actions. Despite its important strengths, curriculum-based measurement does suffer from a key limitation. In stark contrast to either behavioral assessment's or mastery learning's focus on discrete measurement tasks, the assessment task in curriculum-based measurement is global. Although curriculum-based measurement's relatively broad, long-term measurement focus has clear advantages in terms of indexing a student's competence on well-integrated performances, it also creates two disadvantages. First, the measurement system requires longer time periods to reveal growth than do behavioral assessment or mastery learning frameworks. Second, some critics contend that, because of its broad focus, the database provides fewer insights for teachers about exactly how to improve instructional programs. The connection between the assessment and what instructional move to take is not as clear as it is with the other two assessment methods (e.g., Lentz & Kramer, 1993).

Changing times may prompt a shift in curriculum-based measurement's focus. Unfortunately, controversy also exists about the importance of the learning outcomes associated with curriculum-based measurement. For example, curriculum-based measurement relies heavily on paper-and-pencil tasks in math and spelling and one-dimensional assessments in reading. By contrast, current discussions about critical outcomes stress the utility of multidimensional projects that better represent real-life performances. Also, curriculum-based measurement relies on timed assessments, whereby competence is defined in terms of accuracy and fluency. By contrast, some reformers argue that assessments should not be timed—that competence should be conceptualized in terms of the legitimacy of the student's strategic behavior. In addition, with curriculum-based measurement, students complete assessments independently so that the individual's growth can be estimated. This stands in contrast to a new reliance on group assessments in which individuals' capacity to work cooperatively can be determined, but it can be difficult to identify an individual's contribution and level of competence.

In light of recent discussions about the requirements of today's work settings and everyday life, the learning outcomes to which curriculum-based measurement is linked may seem outdated. With curriculum-based measurement, the school's curriculum determines the content and structure of the assessment. Unfortunately, if today's curricula are misguided, as suggested in current critiques, then they may misdirect curriculum-based measurement. Similarly, the key behaviors indexed within curriculum-based measurement have been determined through criterion validity studies to identify which behaviors relate to other, well-established indicators of competence, such as performance on frequently used commercial achievement tests or teacher judgments of competence. In light of recent criticisms about the restricted focus of commercial achievement tests and because of newer conceptualizations of what competent academic performance should look like, these criterion variables may now be problematic.

In any case, although curriculum-based measurement's focus may be out of step with today's reform rhetoric, it remains largely compatible with current practice in schools. When schools redefine their curricula, when teachers reconceptualize the nature of competent academic performance, and when external tests are reshaped to match newer visions of academic competence, curriculum-based measurement will evolve accordingly.

4. Performance Assessment: Definition and Case Study

Definition of Performance Assessment

Performance assessment is a newer variety of assessment designed to forge a tight connection with instruction. The purpose of performance assessment is to direct teachers and students toward important learning outcomes, enabling teachers to design superior instructional plans and effect better student achievement.

According to the U.S. Congress, Office of Technology Assessment (1992), performance assessments have three key features: (1) The assessment tasks require students to construct, rather than select, responses; (2) the assessment formats create opportunities for teachers to observe student behavior on tasks reflecting real-world requirements; and (3) the scoring methods reveal patterns in students' learning and thinking, in addition to the correctness of the students' answers.

Case Study in Instructional Planning

The following case study illustrates the design and application of performance assessment. It relies on a modified performance assessment problem featured in the *Arithmetic Teacher* (Sammons, Kobett, Heiss, & Fennell, 1992). The problem measures massed mathematical concepts that include addition, multiplication, decimals, data analysis, perimeter, area, spatial sense, graphic representation, money, and communication about mathematics. Similar assessments are designed to be used four to six times per year. The duration of the assessment is approximately 50 minutes, and it can be completed individually or in small groups. The problem is anchored in a real-life, age-appropriate situation and represents real applications of mathematics. The following narrative describes the problem to be solved.

A group of five families on your block is going to have a garage sale in which clothes, toys, and books will be sold.

Your family has 12 items to sell and will need 18 square feet to display these items; the Hamletts have 13 items and need 20 square feet; the Phillips, 7 items and 10 square feet; the Thompsons, 15 items and 15 square feet; and the Nelsons, 10 items and 30 square feet. Each family would like to have its own table or cluster of tables to oversee. The rental store tells you that you can rent tables measuring 6 feet by 2.5 feet for $6.00 per day. The garage where the sale will occur is 20 feet by 30 feet. Newspaper advertising costs $11.00 for the first 10 words and $1.50 for each additional word.

1. How many tables will you need? Explain how you got this number.

2. Draw a diagram showing how the tables can be arranged in the garage to allow the customers to move about with at least 4 feet between tables.

3. Write an ad for your sale that includes enough information.

4. How much money do you have to earn from your sale for the families to break even?

As the teacher introduces this problem, she simultaneously explains the scoring rubric she will employ. As shown in Figure 3, the sample scoring rubric, under development by the Wisconsin Performance Assessment Development Project, classifies responses as exemplary, competent, minimal, inadequate, and no attempt. The students are aware of the scoring system and the exact criterion used to determine the possible scores.

Different strategies will produce a correct response to this series of questions, and there is more than one correct set of answers. Not every set of responses, however, is correct. Figures 4, 5, and 6 show three fourth-graders' responses to this problem: The first set of responses is completely correct; the second set of responses shows three of four correct segments; the third set of responses is incorrect. Nevertheless, all three responses are useful for understanding the students' mathematical strategies, understandings, strengths, and weaknesses.

Marlena's work, shown in Figure 4, illustrates a well-organized, sophisticated set of strategies for approaching this problem. It incorporates correct applications of algorithms, which are executed accurately. The explanations for derived answers are clear and well conceptualized and indicate the ability to communicate about mathematics effectively. After inspecting Marlena's work, the teacher, Mrs. Grand, determines

FIGURE 3
Sample Mathematics Scoring Rubric

4 Exemplary Response
4.1 Complete in every way with clear, coherent, unambiguous and insightful explanation
4.2 Shows understanding of underlying mathematical concepts, procedures, and structures
4.3 Examines and satisfies all essential conditions of the problem
4.4 Presents strong supporting arguments with examples and counterexamples as appropriate
4.5 Solution and work is efficient and shows evidence of reflection and checking of work
4.6 Appropriately applies mathematics to the situation

3 Competent Response
3.1 Gives a fairly complete response with reasonably clear explanations
3.2 Shows understanding of underlying mathematical concepts, procedures, and structures
3.3 Examines and satisfies most essential conditions of the problem
3.4 Presents adequate supporting arguments with examples and counterexamples as appropriate
3.5 Solution and work show some evidence of reflection and checking of work
3.6 Appropriately applies mathematics to the situation

2 Minimal Response
2.1 Gives response, but explanations may be unclear or lack detail
2.2 Exhibits minor flaws in underlying mathematical concepts, procedures, and structures
2.3 Examines and satisfies some essential conditions of the problem
2.4 Draws some accurate conclusions, but reasoning may be faulty or incomplete
2.5 Shows little evidence of reflection and checking of work
2.6 Some attempt to apply mathematics to the situation

1 Inadequate Response
1.1 Response is incomplete and explanation is insufficient or not understandable
1.2 Exhibits major flaws in underlying mathematical concepts, procedures, and structures
1.3 Fails to address essential conditions of the problem
1.4 Uses faulty reasoning and draws incorrect conclusions
1.5 Shows no evidence of reflection and checking of work
1.6 Fails to apply mathematics to the situation

0 No attempt
0.1 Provides irrelevant or no response
0.2 Copies part of the problem but does not attempt a solution
0.3 Illegible response

Note: To receive a particular score a significant number of the associated criteria must be met.
Source: Wisconsin School Assessment System (1993).

FIGURE 4
Marlena's Responses to the Performance Assessment Problem

Name : Marlena

1. 1 table : 6' x 2.5' = 15 sq.'

	sq. ft needed	# tables needed.
Thompsons	15	15/15 = ①
Ours	18	18/15 = 1.2 → ②
Phillips	10	10/15 = .67 → ①
Hamletts	20	20/15 = 1.3 → ②
Nelsons	30	30/15 = ②

Total tables needed: 1 + 2 + 1 + 2 + 2 = ⑧
We'll need 8 tables because each table gives 15 sq.'.
2 families need 15 sq.' or less + therefore each need
1 table. 3 families need more than 15 sq.' but no
more than 30 sq.', so they each need 2 tables.
(2 families x 1 table) + (3 families x 2 tables) =
          2   +   6   = 8 tables

2.

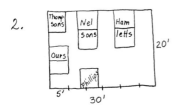

    20'
  5'   30'

3. Garage Sale. Toys, clothes, books. 325 Farm St.
Sat. June 20. 8 am - 2 pm.
    13 words   10 words @ $ 10.00
        + 3 words @
          3 x $1.50   4.50
                $14.50

4. ad costs $ 14.50
    tables cost 8 x $ 6.00 = $42.00 $56.50 need to earn
                                           to break even

FIGURE 5
Jose's Responses to the Performance Assessment Problem

Name: Jose

1. $\overset{3}{2}.5$ Thompsons need 15 ⟶ 1 table
    $\times\ 6$ We need 18   ⟶ 2 tables
    $\overline{15.0}$ Phillips need 10 ⟶ 1 table
         Hamletts need 20 ⟶ 2 tables
         Nelsons need 30 ⟶ 2 tables
                        ⟨8 tables⟩

    Because families that need more than
    15 will need 2 tables

2.

3. June 20. 8-2 p.m. Sale. Toys, clothes,
    books. 325 Farm St.
        11 words $10.00 + 1.50 = $11.50

4. $11.50 + 6 × 8 = 42.00
                   + 11.50
                  ⟨$53.50⟩

FIGURE 6
Freda's Responses to the Performance Assessment Problem

Name: <u>Freda</u>

1. 6 × 5.5 = 150

   thompeone have 15 iteme - 1 table
We have 15 iteme - 1 table
Phillipe have 10 iteme - 1 table
Hamlette have 1E iteme - 1 table

               (5 tablez)

Becauee each table hae an area
oF 150 and each family has no more
than 15 items, each family neebs
1 table.

2.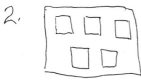

3.   Come to our great garage sale
on June 50. 322 Farm st.
        12 words   10.00
        2 × 1.50   +30.00
               ($40.00)

4. 40.00 + 5 × 6 = 30.00 = (70.00)

that Marlena is competent on the portions of the curriculum represented on this assessment, and she awards Marlena a score of 4. Mrs. Grand decides that Marlena's instruction should now focus on fractions and related concepts and applications.

As shown in Figure 5, Jose has responded to most aspects of the problem in an appropriate, constructive manner. He selects necessary pieces of information and ignores irrelevant parts of the problems. He organizes the information so that his addition and multiplication algorithms are applied to the right information, and his computation is accurate when incorporating whole numbers as well as decimals. He writes a short ad that contains all necessary information, and he determines the costs accurately. Thus, Jose has demonstrated clear strengths in applying many fourth-grade skills within an integrated performance. Nevertheless, Mrs. Grand notices that, although Jose appears to understand the relationship between the dimensions of an object and its corresponding area (as indicated in Part 1 of his answer), his spatial representation of the garage is disorganized and reflects conceptual confusion about area and about the requirements for each family to have its table(s) together. In addition, Jose's explanation for his response in part 1 is inarticulate and does not communicate to others the strategies he employed, as shown in his work. Mrs. Grand awards Jose a score of 2 and decides that Jose's instruction should focus on concrete representations of area and the relationship between area and the dimensions of objects. Jose also requires additional work in verbalizing his mathematics so that he can communicate effectively.

Freda is a student with a diagnosed learning disability who participates in Mrs. Grand's fourth-grade mathematics class. In contrast to Marlena's and Jose's performances, Freda's work, shown in Figure 6, suggests more serious, fundamental misconceptions and difficulties. Although Freda seems to know the formula for calculating area when given the dimensions of an object, as shown in her determination of the area of the display table (i.e., width times length), her work produces a nonsensible answer (i.e., $6 \times 2.5 = 150$ square feet per table). Because Freda accepts this nonsensible answer in Part 1 and attempts to support her answer with an explanation for its derivation, Mrs. Grand infers that Freda lacks concrete understanding about object dimensions, the relationship between an object's dimensions and its area, and number sense when the numbers incorporate decimals. Two additional aspects of Freda's work support this diagnosis: (a) her use of the irrelevant information (i.e., number of display objects rather than square feet) in calculating number of tables needed and (b) her simplistic drawing, which deletes most important information, to represent her spatial plan. An additional problem is revealed by Freda's inarticulate explanation in

Part 1, as well as the substance of her newspaper ad, which contains unnecessary information ("come to our great," "on") and omits critical information (e.g., time, types of items to be sold). Consequently, Mrs. Grand awards Freda a score of 1 and decides that Freda requires conceptual work with concrete objects to remediate misunderstandings about decimals as well as spatial concepts. In addition, Freda needs corrective activities on algorithms involving decimals and instructional activities designed to enhance her capacity to communicate about mathematics.

5. Performance Assessment: Strengths and Limitations

The case study described in Chapter 4 was formulated on the basis of key design features described in the literature. It offers one version of what a teacher's use of performance assessment for instructional planning might look like. In practice, many varieties of performance assessment are described in the literature, and a wide range of methods are implemented today in classrooms. Some are designed deliberately to reflect performance assessment's essential dimensions. Yet, because performance assessment is relatively new, underdeveloped, and yet to be studied systematically, practitioners often are in the undesirable position of interpreting vague design features and operationalizing those features into specific assessments on their own. These assessments take a variety of forms, some of which are closer than others in approximating the conceptual and theoretical underpinnings of performance assessment.

Performance assessment exists more as a vision of what classroom-based assessment methods might strive to achieve than a clearly defined, readily usable assessment technology.

Thus, performance assessment exists more as a vision of what classroom-based assessment methods might strive to achieve than a clearly defined, readily usable assessment technology. Despite its strong conceptual underpinnings, difficult issues in operationalizing this assessment methodology remain. This chapter revisits the seven issues essential to the development of a useful, acceptable assessment methodology and highlights the challenges that developers of performance assessment face in ensuring that performance assessment achieves its potential.

Measuring Important Student Outcomes

As discussed earlier, behavioral assessment's demand for the measurement of discrete, observable behaviors and mastery learning's reliance on a task-analytic framework have steered adherents away from the complex, integrated performances heralded within the current reform movement. On the other hand, critics of curriculum-based measurement, which focuses on broader, better-integrated performances, have pointed to a looser connection between this assessment strategy and implications for instructional programming. In addition, some argue that the methods by which curriculum-based measurement determines its measurement focus (i.e., relying on the school's curriculum and on criterion validity studies) may render current versions less well related to what is important to learn in today's complicated world.

As illustrated by contrasting problems inherent in these assessment traditions, tension exists among (a) designing a measurement system that focuses on an appropriately sized instructional domain (i.e., a small enough chunk for students to learn); (b) designing an assessment strategy that mirrors valued, authentic, real-world performance in a world where values may change rapidly; and (c) keeping the connection between a manageable instructional chunk and that real-world performance assessment tight. One of the clear challenges for performance assessment is to resolve this dilemma. Performance assessment's deliberate focus on authentic performances that require students to integrate many subskills within age-appropriate, real-world contexts creates a potential vehicle for addressing this dilemma. In resolving this dilemma, both theoretical discussions and empirical investigations regarding core sets of outcomes are needed. A clear set of outcomes to guide the selection of assessment domains and points of focus will help avoid unmanageably long lists of assessment domains. On the other hand, clear guidelines also can help avoid the use of fewer assessment targets that are not closely related to critical outcomes.

Such a core set of critical assessment targets will have to meet several key tests. First, it should reflect current visions of competent, important real-world performances. Second, it should connect meaningfully with specific instructional methods that can be managed realistically within school settings. Third, as suggested by community programs for today's students with severe cognitive disabilities and by the renewed federal interest in vocational programming, a core set of critical outcomes should vary with individual capabilities and overall goals. This may raise sticky questions about (a) the extent to which students with different types of learning outcomes may require alternative curricula and instructional methods or (b) when in a student's educational career the selection of appropriate learning outcomes, which places students on different learning tracks, should occur. Finally, a core set of critical outcomes should be monitored to ensure its continued relevance to the rapidly changing demands of the workplace and everyday life.

Addressing the Three Purposes of Instructional Planning

As illustrated in the performance assessment case study, Mrs. Grand was able to identify useful diagnostic planning decisions for Jose and Freda on the basis of the assessment she conducted. Given the rhetoric surrounding performance assessment, however, we also should expect decisions about placement and formative evaluation to be forthcoming on the basis of the assessment information. In fact, for Marlena, Mrs. Grand did formulate a placement decision indicating that the student needed to progress to instruction on fractions and related concepts and applications. Unfortunately, careful scrutiny of the case study does not reveal the basis for such a decision. Although it was clear that Marlena had achieved sufficient mastery of the massed concepts embedded in the assessment problem, it was not clear how Mrs. Grand identified fractions as the most appropriate focus for subsequent instruction. Perhaps Marlena did require such an instructional focus, but it is equally possible that Marlena had already mastered conceptual and applied information about fractions and needed a more advanced topic of study, or that she required an instructional focus on massed concepts and applications involving subtraction and division. Because performance assessment is not conceptually oriented toward instructional hierarchies, and because an alternative framework has not emerged to address instructional placement issues, additional work is required to identify how performance assessment can be used to formulate placement decisions.

In addition, the case study does not illustrate how formative evaluation decisions might be made. Ideally, alternate forms of the problem presented in the case study could include the same massed concepts in equivalent assessments administered over time, thereby providing information about individual student progress. However, quantitative methods for scoring performances and qualitative methods for describing this progress are not yet available. Methods for designing alternate forms of relatively complex problems also need to be developed. Initial work suggests that it may be difficult to achieve comparability of assessments when different, complex problems are involved (Baxter, Shavelson, Goldman, & Pine, 1992; Shavelson, Baxter, & Pine, 1992). Although performance assessment offers the promise of addressing all three assessment purposes simultaneously, specific methods for addressing these three concerns are yet to be developed.

Providing Detailed Descriptions of Student Performance with an Immediate, Clear Link to Specific Instructional Decisions

When performance assessment addresses a variety of concepts within age-appropriate, real-world situations, it allows teachers to formulate a picture of student performance across skills and identify the strategies a student employs to address a complicated problem. Ideally, this dual focus on skills and strategies should yield rich, detailed descriptions of student performance that can provide immediate, clear links to specific instructional decisions. Using these types of information, a teacher may identify what skill to teach as well as how to teach it.

However, teachers vary considerably in their ability to (a) accurately identify student competencies on different skills, (b) insightfully note information about students' strategic behavior, and (c) relate these descriptions to specific instructional techniques. Research (e.g., Fuchs, Fuchs, Hamlett, & Stecker, 1990, 1991) suggests that all three of these tasks may be difficult for teachers, even when the assessment method and the conceptual framework for learning are simpler than with performance assessment. With curriculum-based measurement, for example, research suggests that teachers find it difficult to generate accurate skills profiles on the basis of assessment that addresses massed concepts (e.g., Fuchs et al., 1990). Because of this difficulty, some assessment developers have moved to automatic, computerized strategies for generating reliable profiles of student competence. Even when provided with skills profiles that identify student problems, teachers find it difficult to connect the problems to corrective instructional strategies (e.g., Fuchs et al., 1991). Because of this difficulty, curriculum-based measurement typically is used in conjunction with human or computerized instructional consultation methods.

A professional development agenda to help teachers meet the challenge of using performance assessment is required.

After specific techniques for creating performance assessments have been identified, developers must study the extent to which teachers can (a) perform the diagnostic strategies necessary to generate rich, detailed descriptions of student performance and (b) make meaningful connections between diagnostic classifications and corrective instructional techniques. Based on this, they must identify specific strategies to

---

assist teachers in using performance assessment to enhance instructional planning.

Compatibility with Many Instructional Models

Nothing inherent in the philosophy or the initial versions of performance assessment limits the variety of instructional approaches available to teachers. Some of the reform movement rhetoric, however, does pressure teachers to merge authentic assessment with the exclusive use of constructivist teaching approaches. Because of the lack of empirical studies investigating the efficacy of these methods, teachers are cautioned to experiment with a variety of methods as they implement performance—or any other form of assessment—with students with serious learning problems.

Feasibility

As illustrated in the case study presented in Chapter 4, performance assessment can require large amounts of teacher time to (a) design and administer assessments and (b) carefully scrutinize student performances to identify accurate learning patterns and connect those patterns to corrective teaching strategies. Performance assessment developers need to address constraints on teacher time—especially in light of increasing student caseloads (Research for Better Schools, 1988) and increasing diversity of student skills (Jenkins, Jewell, Leceister, Jenkins, & Troutner, 1990; Pallas, Natriello, & McDill, 1989).

In addition, planning decisions formulated on the basis of performance assessment can lead to a complicated instructional setting in which different students are working on different content in different ways. The case study illustrated how the same assessment produced three different instructional plans. It is easy to imagine how developing plans to simultaneously address the needs of 20 to 30 students can quickly lead some teachers to reject the assessment model—unless assessment developers solve the problem of how to implement performance assessment-based plans within the constraints of everyday classroom life.

A similar problem exists with curriculum-based measurement: The assessment system often leads teachers to introduce different intervention strategies for different students at different times. Over the years, it became evident that, unless the curriculum-based measurement developers could identify feasible ways for teachers to implement the variety of instruction called for, teachers would reject the method. In response to this problem, developers have designed peer-mediated teaching methods to help implement the instruction within general education classrooms (e.g., Fuchs, Fuchs, Hamlett, Phillips, & Bentz, 1994). The developers of performance assessment will have to address this issue as well.

Communicating the Goals of Learning to Teachers and Students

A much-discussed advantage of performance assessment is that what teachers and students see on assessments corresponds closely to the desired goals of instruction. Therefore, teachers should be able to use performance assessments to direct their instruction. Moreover, to the extent that the scoring rubrics are clear, concrete, and visible, pupils should be able to use the assessments to establish personal learning goals and seek assistance in achieving those goals. Communicating clearly to teachers and students about what is important to teach and learn is of great concern to performance assessment developers. As they define specific methods, we should expect to see clearly articulated goals and scoring criteria to assist teachers and students in translating the assessments into everyday learning activities.

Generating Accurate, Meaningful Information

As specified by Linn, Baker, and Dunbar (1991), developers need to rethink the technical criteria by which the quality of educational assessments is judged. These researchers proposed that performance assessments be evaluated by the following criteria:

- Evidence about the intended and unintended effects of the assessments on the ways teachers and students spend their time and think about the goals of education.

- Fairness of the assessments for different populations of learners.

- Accuracy of generalizations from the specific assessment tasks to broader domains of achievement.

- Consistency of the content of the assessment with current understandings of important features of the domain of knowledge.

- Comprehensiveness of the content coverage of the assessment.

- Meaningfulness of the assessment to students.

- Acceptable costs and efficiency associated with the methods.

In specifying these criteria, Linn and colleagues (1991) have articulated an important research program for performance assessment developers. At present, it seems clear that reliability problems need to be addressed. Moreover, little is known about how well existing forms of performance assessment satisfy the criteria.

Conclusion

Performance assessment's emphasis on complexity and authenticity reflects dissatisfaction with the strong focus of standardized achievement tests on basic, factual content and multiple-choice formats, as well as with the influence such tests have had on directing everyday learning activities. It represents a vision that can shape the future direction of classroom-based assessment. Unfortunately, performance assessment requires much additional development and scrutiny before it can fulfill its promise.

Performance assessment represents a vision that can shape the future direction of classroom-based assessment.

As described by Steve Forman, a project officer with the National Assessment of Education Progress (NAEP) during an interview with *The Wall Street Journal* (Trost, 1992), the testing pendulum "swings back and forth.... Twenty-three years ago, NAEP was using open-ended, hands-on types of exercises ... then the pendulum swung back to multiple choice, and now it's swinging back the other way." To avoid another pendulum swing back toward traditional testing models, performance assessment developers need to define clear sets of methods that practitioners can use profitably and efficiently. They also need to document related effects empirically and carefully—using rules of evidence that can satisfy a wide range of audiences.

References

Anderson-Inman, L., Walker, H. M., & Purcell, J. (1984). Promoting the transfer of skills across settings: Transenvironmental programming for handicapped students in the mainstream. In W. L. Heward, T. E. Heron, D. S. Hill, & J. Trap-Porter (Eds.), *Focus on behavior analysis in education* (pp. 17–37). Columbus, OH: Merrill.

Archbald, D. A., & Newmann, F. M. (1988). *Beyond standardized testing: Assessing academic achievement in the secondary school*. Reston, VA: National Association of Secondary School Principals.

Baer, D. M., Wolf, M. M., & Risley, T. R. (1987). Some still-current dimensions of applied behavior analysis. *Journal of Applied Behavior Analysis, 20*, 313–327.

Baxter, G. P., Shavelson, R. J., Goldman, S. R., & Pine, J. (1992). Evaluation of procedure-based scoring for hands-on science assessment. *Journal of Educational Measurement, 29*, 1–17.

Bloom, B. S. (1976). *Human characteristics and school learning*. New York: McGraw-Hill.

Block, J. H., & Burns, R. B. (1976). Mastery learning. In L. S. Schulman (Ed.), *Review of research in education* (Vol. 4, pp. 3–49). Itasca, IL: Peacock.

Carroll, J. B. (1963). A model for school learning. *Teachers College Record, 64*, 723–733.

Dornbusch, S. M., & Scott, W. R. (1975). *Evaluation and the exercise of authority*. San Francisco: Jossey-Bass.

Fleming, M., & Chambers, B. (1983). Teacher-made tests: Windows to the classroom. In W. E. Hathaway (Ed.), *New directions for testing and measurement: Testing in the schools* (pp. 29–38). San Francisco: Jossey-Bass.

Fuchs, L. S., & Deno, S. L. (1991). Paradigmatic distinctions between instructionally relevant measurement models. *Exceptional Children, 57*, 488–501.

Fuchs, L. S., Fuchs, D., Hamlett, C. L., & Ferguson, C. (1992). Effects of expert system consultation within curriculum-based measurement using a reading maze task. *Exceptional Children, 58,* 436–450.

Fuchs, L. S., Fuchs, D., Hamlett, C. L., Phillips, N. R., & Bentz, J. (1994). Classwide curriculum-based measurement: Helping general educators meet the challenge of student diversity. *Exceptional Children, 60,* 518–537.

Fuchs, L. S., Fuchs, D., Hamlett, C. L., & Stecker, P. M. (1990). The role of skills analysis in curriculum-based measurement in math. *School Psychology Review, 19,* 6–22.

Fuchs, L. S., Fuchs, D., Hamlett, C. L., & Stecker, P. M. (1991). Effects of curriculum-based measurement and consultation on teacher planning and student achievement in mathematics operations. *American Educational Research Journal, 28,* 617–641.

Fuchs, L. S., Tindal, G., & Fuchs, D. (1986). Effects of mastery learning on student achievement. *Journal of Educational Research, 79,* 286–291.

Jenkins, J. R., Jewell, M., Leceister, N., Jenkins, L., & Troutner, N. (1990, April). *Development of a school building model for educating handicapped and at risk students in general education classrooms.* Paper presented at the annual meeting of the American Educational Research Association, Boston.

Kratochwill, T. R., & Shapiro, E. S. (1988). Introduction: Conceptual foundations of behavioral assessment in schools. In E. S. Shapiro & T. R. Kratochwill (Eds.), *Behavioral assessment in schools: Conceptual foundations and practical applications* (pp. 1–13). New York: Guilford.

Lentz, F. E., & Kramer, J. J. (1993). Academic skill assessment: An evaluation of the role and function of curriculum-based measurements. In J. J. Kramer (Ed.), *Curriculum-based measurement* (pp. 105–122). Lincoln: Buros Institute of Mental Measurements, University of Nebraska.

Linn, R. L. (1991). Dimensions of thinking: Implications for testing. In B. F. Jones & L. Idol (Eds.), *Educational values and cognitive instruction: Implications for reform* (pp. 179–208). Hillsdale, NJ: Erlbaum.

Linn, R. L., Baker, E. L., & Dunbar, S. B. (1991, November). Complex, performance-based assessment: Expectations and validation criteria. *Educational Researcher,* pp. 15–21.

Natriello, G., & Dornbusch, S. M. (1984). *Teacher evaluative standards and student effort.* New York: Longman.

Nitko, A. J. (1989). Designing tests that are integrated with instruction. In R. L. Linn (Ed.), *Educational measurement* (3rd ed., pp. 447–474). New York: American Council on Education, Macmillan.

Pallas, A. M., Natriello, G., & McDill, E. L. (1989). The changing nature of the disadvantaged population: Current dimensions and future trends. *Educational Researcher, 18*(5), 16–22.

Performance Assessment Development Project. (1993). Mathematics Scoring Rubric. Unpublished draft. Madison, WI: Author.

Research for Better Schools. (1988). *Special education in America's cities: A descriptive study.* Philadelphia: Author.

Sammons, K. B., Kobett, B., Heiss, J., & Fennell, F. S. (1992, February). Linking instruction and assessment in the mathematics classroom. *Arithmetic Teacher,* pp. 11–15.

Shavelson, R. J., Baxter, G. P., & Pine, J. (1992). Performance assessments: Political rhetoric and measurement reality. *Educational Researcher, 21*(4), 22–27.

Shepard, L. A. (1989, April). Why we need better assessments. *Educational Leadership, 46.*

Stiggins, R. J., Griswald, M., & Green, K. R. (1988, April). *Measuring thinking skills through classroom assessment.* Paper presented at the 1988 annual meeting of the National Council on Measurement in Education, New Orleans.

Tawney, J. W., & Gast, D. L. (1984). *Single subject research in special education.* Columbus, OH: Merrill.

Tindal, G., Fuchs, L. S., Fuchs, D., Shinn, M. R., Deno, S. L., & Germann, G. (1985). Empirical validation of criterion-referenced tests. *Journal of Educational Research, 78,* 203–209.

Trost, C. (1992, November 4). Report criticizes traditional methods of math testing and offers new models. *The Wall Street Journal.*

U.S. Congress, Office of Technology Assessment. (1992, February). *Testing in American schools: Asking the right questions* (OTA-SET-519). Washington, DC: U.S. Government Printing Office. (ED 340 770)

White, O. R. (1984). Descriptive analysis of extant research literature concerning skill generalization and the severely/profoundly handicapped. In M. Boer (Ed.), *Investigating the problem of skill generalization: Literature review* (pp. 1–19). Seattle: University of Washington, Washington Research Organization.

Wiggins, G. (1989). A true test: Toward more authentic and equitable assessment. *Phi Delta Kappan, 70,* 703–713.